Search and Rescue Dogs

by Marie Brandle

Bullfrog Books

Ideas for Parents and Teachers

Bullfrog Books let children practice reading informational text at the earliest reading levels. Repetition, familiar words, and photo labels support early readers.

Before Reading

- Discuss the cover photo. What does it tell them?

- Look at the picture glossary together. Read and discuss the words.

Read the Book

- "Walk" through the book and look at the photos. Let the child ask questions. Point out the photo labels.

- Read the book to the child, or have him or her read independently.

After Reading

- Prompt the child to think more. Ask: Did you know about search and rescue dogs before reading this book? What more would you like to learn about them?

Bullfrog Books are published by Jump!
5357 Penn Avenue South
Minneapolis, MN 55419
www.jumplibrary.com

Library of Congress Cataloging-in-Publication Data

Names: Brandle, Marie, 1989– author.
Title: Search and rescue dogs / by Marie Brandle.
Description: Bullfrog books [edition].
Minneapolis: Jump!, Inc., [2022]
Series: Dogs on duty | Includes index.
Audience: Ages 5–8
Identifiers: LCCN 2021014965 (print)
LCCN 2021014966 (ebook)
ISBN 9781645279310 (hardcover)
ISBN 9781645279327 (paperback)
ISBN 9781645279334 (ebook)
Subjects: LCSH: Service dogs—Juvenile literature.
Rescue dogs—Juvenile literature.
Classification: LCC SF428.73 .B73 2022 (print)
LCC SF428.73 (ebook) | DDC 636.7/0886—dc23
LC record available at https://lccn.loc.gov/2021014965
LC ebook record available at https://lccn.loc.gov/2021014966

Editor: Eliza Leahy
Designer: Molly Ballanger

Photo Credits: Figure8Photos/iStock, cover; cynoclub/iStock, 1, 12; chrisbrignell/Shutterstock, 3; Dale A Stork/Shutterstock, 4; Philartphace/iStock, 5, 23tr; Dan Edwards/Dreamstime, 6–7, 23br; ZUMA Press, Inc./Alamy, 8–9, 23bl; Jochen Tack/imageBROKER/SuperStock, 10–11, 23tl, 23bm; Michal Fludra/Alamy, 13; Belish/Dreamstime, 14–15; Belish/Shutterstock, 16–17, 22br, 23tm; Serge Mouraret/Alamy, 18; Biosphoto/SuperStock, 19; ITAR-TASS News Agency/Alamy, 20–21; Jim Parkin/Shutterstock, 22tl; home for heroes/Shutterstock, 22tr; Massimo Todaro/Shutterstock, 22bl; Eric Isselee/Shutterstock, 24.

Printed in the United States of America at Corporate Graphics in North Mankato, Minnesota.

Table of Contents

To the Rescue!

This puppy is in training. Why?

IN TRAINING

He will have an important job.

He will rescue people!

Search and rescue dogs have good noses.

They use them to sniff.

This dog found
a person's scent.

She follows the smell.

There was an earthquake.

People are stuck.

This dog searches for them.

This rescue dog can swim well.

He wears a life jacket.

life jacket

He jumps in the water!

13

A person is stuck
in the snow.

A rescue dog helps!

handler

She found someone.

Woof! Woof!

This lets her
handler know.

This rescue dog works on a boat.

18

helicopter

This one flies
in a helicopter.

These dogs work hard.
They help in many ways!

On the Job

Search and rescue dogs have many jobs. Take a look at some of them!

They search for people who are lost in the wild.

They help find people after earthquakes.

They rescue people in the water.

They search for people in snow after avalanches.

Picture Glossary

earthquake
A shaking of a part of Earth's surface that can cause great damage.

handler
A person who trains or controls an animal.

rescue
To save from danger.

scent
A smell that is left by someone or something.

searches
Explores or examines thoroughly in order to find someone or something.

sniff
To smell by taking short breaths in through the nose.

Index

To Learn More

Finding more information is as easy as 1, 2, 3.

❶ Go to www.factsurfer.com

❷ Enter "searchandrescuedogs" into the search box.

❸ Choose your book to see a list of websites.